For Barbie

Glider Pilot

James Webster

Illustrated by Peter Dennis

M

Macmillan Education

1

Truth is stranger than fiction. So they say. But a lot of strange things happen in books. Look at James Bond. You know what he did.

Yet he didn't. He didn't really do anything. It all happened in the books. Fiction. Not like my story. That's true. Every word of it.

I'm dead. I'm a ghost. Or I should be. But of course I'm not. I'm sitting here writing down what happened. Yes. Truth is a whole lot stranger than fiction. Especially when it all happens to you.

What I did broke records. It nearly broke my neck. Why it didn't is still a bit of a mystery. To me, at any rate. Maybe you can work it out. Why am I still alive?

It sounds something like a James Bond story. A hunt for a diamond. A big one. But this was a diamond in the sky. A long way up.

You don't understand, do you? Perhaps I'd better start right at the beginning.

2

You never forget your first flight. Not in a glider.
Not in a plane without an engine.

I went to have a look round a gliding club. Just to
watch. Gliders were floating about in the sky. They
looked like huge birds. Very nice, I thought. But
I was just looking.

Then they offered me a joy-ride. Well, I had to say
yes, didn't I? I didn't want to seem scared.

So I let them strap me in this glider. It was
old-fashioned, with an open cockpit and big struts.
It didn't look too safe.

The pilot showed me the instruments. One for your
speed. One for your height. And one to tell you if
the glider was going up or down. I had more things
in my car than that, I thought.

One man held the wings level. Another hooked us onto
a long cable. At the other end was a powerful winch.
The pilot checked his controls. My heart began to
thump. We were ready for takeoff.

We bumped along the ground. Then the pilot moved th
stick back. We shot up into the air. You know those
switchbacks at the fair? That's what it felt like.

At last we dropped the cable. Things slowed down
a bit. I got my breath back. It was all so quiet.
So calm. Fantastic. Just like being a bird.

I looked round. It all seemed so different. The
clouds were alive. The sun was alive. Everything was
alive. More alive than ever before. Things on the
ground looked small. They didn't matter any more.
We were free. Free as air.

Slowly we floated down. The pilot turned towards
the club. He flew faster. My eyes were watering with
the wind. The ground came rushing up to meet us.

The glider's one wheel skimmed the grass. A bump.
A rumble. Then we were down. My flight had ended.
I looked at my watch. Three minutes? Is that all
it had been?

Funny. Half of me was still a bit scared. The other
half couldn't wait to go up again. That half won.
I joined the club on the spot. I was hooked.

4

3

Learning to fly looked easy. All you had was this stick between your legs. That made the glider climb or dive. It also made it bank and turn.

Pedals worked the rudder. A lever worked the air brakes. And that was that. No gears or clutch to worry about. Yes, it looked easy.

But it wasn't. Not once you were up in the air. That glider had a mind of her own. She skidded about all over the sky. When I used my hands I forgot about my feet. When I used my feet I forgot about my hands.

I thought I'd never learn.

Those short three minute flights didn't help. Then one day we flew into some air that was going up. "Lift", as they called it.

We flew round and round in this lift. Suddenly I found I could do it. I was flying. More than that, I was climbing. The ground was getting smaller and smaller. I looked at the instruments. 2,000 feet − without an engine! How much higher could we go? I shivered with excitement. And cold.

Wisps of white floated by. We were touching the clouds. I forgot the cold and gazed down. The view took my breath away. I felt like a god.

Browns. Yellows. Different greens splashed about. Red dabs for roof tops. A giant paint box lay below.

Then my instructor took over. He wanted to show me something. We slowed up. Everything went quiet. Suddenly that paint box was spinning round. I didn't feel like a god any more. I felt sick.

I learnt how to spin. And how to get out of a spin. That was the important bit. I learnt how to take off and land. Without too many bumps. But I didn't find lift again for a long time. I just thought about it.

I thought about the clouds. What was it like, flying inside them? I had climbed to 2,000 feet. What was it like at 20,000 feet? Flying blind.

Once I saw a thunderstorm in the distance. I was waiting to fly. "What's it like, flying inside that?" I asked the instructor. "Stop dreaming," he said. "You've not even flown solo yet."

But I had. I flew solo every night. He was right. I did a lot of dreaming.

6

4

My dream came true. I flew solo. Three long minutes alone in the sky. Then I went up again. That flight lasted 15 minutes. I was beginning to learn.

I learnt how to look for lift. Mostly it was under clouds. The fat, white clouds you see on a summer's day. They sucked you upwards.

Sometimes there was lift over hills. The wind had to be blowing the right way. When it was, you could fly up and down in front of a hill. You could keep going for a long time like that.

One gliding test is to fly for five hours. It's not as hard as it sounds. Not the flying part. You wait till the wind is blowing the right way. Then you hover over the hills like a hawk. Hour after hour.

The hard part is to think what you're doing all the time. You've got to keep your eyes open. The glider does most of the flying for you. But you can't go to sleep.

I did my five hours in February. It was cold. Freezing cold. But the wind was just right.

I flew up and down in front of a hill. My glider
didn't have an open cockpit. So I thought I'd be
warm. I wasn't. I got colder and colder. You need
lots of clothes for this kind of flying. That's
something else I learnt.

The sun came out. Sometimes it was right in my eyes.
I didn't mind. At last it was a bit warmer. I let
the glider fly itself. Now I could rub my hands
together.

Then a cold black shadow slid into the cockpit.
I looked up and gasped. Another glider came out of
the sun. Straight at me. I grabbed the controls and
threw my glider sideways.

A wingtip flashed past my head. I ducked. For a
second I saw the other pilot's face. He was
screaming something at me. Then he had gone.

We had missed by a coat of paint. I was warm now.
Sweating. From then on I kept my eyes skinned.
Gliders can hit each other. Very easily. I'd nearly
found that out the hard way.

Oh yes. I was learning all right.

5

Planes can tow gliders into the air. It's much better
than the winch. Not so steep. And you can go a lot
higher of course. But you need to watch out. When
you're learning it's easy to get lost.

That happened to me. I couldn't find the club. I had
to land somewhere so I picked a nice big field. Then
I found some lift. I tried to climb. No luck.

But now I was in trouble. The wind had taken me away
from my big field. I couldn't get back to it. Below
lay a steep valley. Full of trees and rocks. I began
to panic. Then I saw a tiny field to my left. It was
horribly small. But anything was better than crashing
into those trees and rocks.

I banked steeply. The ground rushed up. Hedges lay
in wait. I landed with a bang and the glider stopped
dead. That steep slope had saved me.

I got my breath back and walked to a farm cottage.
An old man with a hook for an arm opened the door.
He scowled and waved it at me. Funny, I thought.

Proudly I told him about my forced landing. He waved
that hook in my face. He swore. Then he called me
a liar. He'd been a pilot once. So why hadn't he
heard my engine?

I told him why. I showed him the glider. He shook
his head. "You must be mad," he said. "Going up
without an engine. How will you get home?"

He soon saw how. A long trailer came from the club.
We took the glider to bits. In it went. Almost.
It didn't fit too well. I had to hold on to the tail.
I could hardly stand up by the time we got back.

Some funny things happen when you land in fields.
One farmer got me drunk. Another time my glider was
attacked by cows. A whole herd of them.

That was awful. They split up. Then they came at the
glider from all sides. They rubbed against the tail.
They licked the nose. They even jumped over the wings.
I was running round, screaming at them. Waving
my arms at them. Yelling for help.

No one heard. It was an hour before help came. I was
in a bit of a state by then. Still, things could
have been worse. Those cows could have been bulls.

12

6

Winter came again. There were some beautiful clouds about. Snow clouds. One day I found lift under them. I went on climbing. Slowly the ground faded away.

I was in a new world. Grey, cool and silent. A world of strange feelings. The world of clouds.

This glider had blind flying instruments. But I hadn't flown blind before. Soon I got into trouble. The glider nose-dived out of the cloud. I looked around. Where was the airfield?

Where was the ground? I couldn't see a thing. It was snowing hard. I tried to fly straight. Then I saw something. Just for a second. House tops. I was over some small town. Then more snow blotted it out again.

I was coming down very fast now. And still flying blind. I thought about those house tops. Where was I going to land?

Suddenly the ground loomed out of the snow. I gasped with relief. By sheer luck I was over a golf course. Seconds later I had landed. Right on a green.

A man was watching me. He waited for my glider to stop. Then he hit his ball and walked away. Just as if nothing had happened. He didn't even look back. Funny people, these golfers.

After that I kept away from snow clouds. I waited for better weather. Then I learnt to fly blind in small clouds. It didn't matter if I dived out of those. I could see where I was.

I did more and more cloud flying. I loved being up in that secret silence. I began to fly high. High enough to win cups.

The first time I got to 10,000 feet I felt as if I had climbed Everest. I was shouting with joy. My wings sparkled in the sun. The ground looked like a map. From this height I could fly for ever.

For ever? A quarter of an hour later I had landed. I only just made it back to the airfield. The wings still sparkled. No wonder. They had ice all over them.

Ice does things to a glider. It makes you come down very quickly. Very quickly indeed.

But just how quickly I had yet to find out.

7

I had a new dream now. Diamonds. Diamonds in the sky.
You could win one of them by gliding 300 kilometres.
You wore it on your gliding badge. But you had to say
where you were going to land before you took off.

300 kilometres is a long way. It took some doing.
At first I tried flying downwind. You went faster.
I made for the East coast. But I always got lost.
Once I came out of the clouds over some flat ground.
Very flat. Then I saw ships. I was over the sea.

I just got back to the coast. Then I landed. At the
wrong place, of course. So I didn't get a diamond.
But I did get a swim. I had my swimming trunks in
the bottom of the cockpit.

In the end I got my diamond. But that wasn't the one
I dreamt about now. Oh no. There was a much better
one. The Height diamond. You had to climb about
17,000 feet to win that. The tow up didn't count. So
you needed to fly even higher. Perhaps 20,000 feet.

20,000 feet. Yes. That was the diamond I dreamt
about. The Height diamond.

I didn't just dream about cloud flying. Sometimes
I day-dreamed as well. I looked out of the window.
I saw a cloud. Then I was away. Climbing up in it.
In my mind.

When I flew I watched every cloud. Even when I was
instructing. That got me into trouble.

We were up in the trainer. The one I had learnt in.
Suddenly we hit a downdraught. I didn't notice for
a moment. My head was in the clouds.

I grabbed the controls. But now we were low. Low and
slow. That means trouble when you're gliding.
I could see it coming.

We went right through the top of a big tree. Then we
staggered on towards the field. We almost made it.
But there was this fence in the way. That was a pity.

No one was hurt. But now we had a big hole in the
bottom of the cockpit. That taught me a lesson.
Diamonds in the sky? I was lucky not to see stars.

For the next few weeks I had a lot of time to
day-dream. I had that hole in the glider to mend.

8

There are competitions for gliders. Mostly races to places and back again. You carry a camera and take photographs. They show where you've been. You hope.

I went in for a competition. I was going to fly the fastest club glider. Then someone broke it. The day before the competition. Think how I felt.

Now I had to fly another club glider. It was much older. And a lot slower. But it was better than nothing. I still had a chance.

It wasn't much of a chance. The first race was to a place upwind. It was hard work in this old glider. I kept getting blown back. Soon I was on my own. And lost, of course.

There was something funny about this glider. The nose kept dropping. I had to keep pulling back on the stick. All the time.

I didn't worry about it. I had too much to do. Where was I? What was that town? Where was the best lift? I was getting low, too.

You push your luck in competitions. You fly on when you should land. That's what I did. I got lower and lower.

Then I saw this cricket pitch. So I landed. That was nearly a mistake. The grass was so smooth I could hardly stop. I went all over the place.

The players weren't too pleased, either. Pushing your luck they said, as I stopped by the stumps. But they didn't know just how far I had pushed it.

That glider was a death-trap. Someone had torn a bit of the tail. Right inside. No one noticed. Every time I pulled back on the stick the tail tore just a little bit more. In the end I could have dived into the ground.

A parachute wasn't much good at that kind of height. For the rest of the competition I kept to the clouds. They were safer. Or so I thought.

All the time I was looking for cloud nine. The one with a diamond hidden inside it.

I didn't win that competition of course. I was always getting lost. But I met a lot of nice people, landing in strange places.

18

9

The years went by. I had my own glider now. But
I still didn't have that other diamond.

This glider was much better than the first ones
I flew. It even had oxygen. Every time I took off
I hoped I would need it. But I didn't.

Then one day the sky looked good. Very good. I had
a low launch. That was good, too. I didn't need to
climb so high now to win my diamond.

One cloud was bigger than the rest. And blacker.
I flew under it. Up I went. Raindrops pinged off my
wings. The whole sky seemed black as ink.

Thunder rumbled. Fingers of cloud hung down all
round me. Just like a ghostly hand. Suddenly it
gripped the glider. It dragged me inside.

For one moment I thought of getting out. While I
could. It was so dark. So quiet. So smooth and evil.
Only my instruments told me how fast I was climbing.
Then a rattle like gunfire made me jump. Hailstones.
Big ones.

The hail stopped. The cloud got blacker. The lift
got stronger. It went right off the clock. There was
enough power in this cloud to rip my glider apart.
Yet the air was silky smooth.

It all happened so quickly. There was no time to turn
on the oxygen. I was up to 17,500 feet in seconds.
Out of the side of the cloud. Then I came hurtling
down again. The ice on my wings made sure of that.
But I'd done it. I won my diamond.

I rubbed at the icy perspex. The sides of my
thundercloud towered above me. A sheet of grey cloud
lay below. A sandwich of silence. Beautiful.

Into cloud. Out again. There was the airfield.
I relaxed in the sun and silence. Suddenly I sat up.
Total silence. No ticking from the little box that
records the flight. And shows the height.

I'd forgotten to switch it on.

I laughed as I landed. Well, it was better than
crying. I had waited years for that climb. For my
Height diamond. I'd done it at last. But I couldn't
prove it. As someone said, I was really switched off
that day.

10

Women fly gliders as well as men. Take that any way
you like. I know a woman who flies them better.
A lot better.

Barbie is another pilot who should be dead. Her story
is part of mine. You'll see why later. And she wasn't
even thinking about diamonds.

Barbie had a winch launch. Then she found that she
couldn't drop the cable. It had jammed. A one in
a million chance. But it happened to her.

They cut the cable away from the winch. So Barbie
was left with 400 metres dangling from her glider.
It shuddered like a great wounded bird. It dived.
It twisted. It turned. But Barbie couldn't get free.

The cable dragged across some power wires. There was
a dreadful flash. Luckily her glider was made of
wood. It was still all right. But now it was falling out of
the sky. Faster and faster.

The awful part was that I was watching. I knew what
would happen. But I couldn't do a thing.

One wing dropped. The glider was going to spin. Now Barbie was as good as dead. No one gets out of a spin that low. And Barbie knew all about spins.

She saw the grass blur and the trees coming. But she never gave up. She went on fighting. At the very last second the wings flicked level. Just above the ground. Coolly she pulled off a perfect landing.

Like she said, never give up. Ever. One day I was going to remember those words. But what a pilot.

Barbie was OK. She went on flying as if nothing had happened. Just for the fun of it. She wasn't bothered about diamonds. Not diamonds in the sky.

But I was. That Height diamond bothered me. I had got it. Yet I hadn't got it. If you see what I mean. Would I ever get another chance?

If I did, I told myself, I'd go really high. Half-way to heaven. But what chance was there? Big clouds don't come along that often.

Not on the days when you're flying. Only when you're safe at work. That's part of the game. Ask any glider pilot. God's law, they call it. Or something like that.

11

I had a new glider. Sailplane is a better word.
A real beauty. She was made of fibreglass, not wood.
Slim. Long, smooth wings, and a high tail.

She was streamlined for speed. Even the landing
wheel retracted. Less drag, more speed. Great.

I tried her out. She was harder to fly. But she
whispered along at ninety without a sound. You
hardly knew you were moving. So you needed to keep
an eye on the ASI.* Especially when landing.

On my third flight I got far too low. Then I had to
put the wheel down in a hurry. After that I was
busy watching the speed.

It seemed OK as I touched down. Then all hell was let
loose. Bangs. Crashes. Thumps. It was a terrible
landing.

I felt as if I was sitting on the ground. I nearly
was. The wheel had retracted. I hadn't had time to
lock it as I landed. My face went red.

*Air Speed Indicator

That was a stupid thing to do. There was no damage.
Just a few scratches. But I had to buy a lot of beer
in the bar that night.

Now I had two week's holiday. I spent them at the
club. It was a good chance to do some more flying
in my new sailplane.

You weren't allowed to go far in a new glider. You
had to get used to it before you risked landing in
a field. So I stayed near the club.

All the same, I tried the sailplane out in cloud.
She was fine. But you had to watch that speed. If
you got out of control you'd be in trouble. You'd
be doing VNE* in seconds.

VNE is as fast as you are allowed to go. About 200
kph in this sailplane. If you fly any faster you
can strain the plane. If you fly a lot faster it may
break up. The wings can come off. Yes, I was going
to have to watch that speed in cloud.

At the end of a week I had to go off for the day.
I had to see my publishers. As I left, big black
clouds were forming. I knew it, I thought.

*Velocity Never Exeed

12

That day was murder. I kept looking out of the window. The clouds got bigger and bigger. Blacker and blacker. Little drops of rain came down. They glittered in the sun like diamonds. Height diamonds.

On the way back there was a thunderstorm. A real cloudburst. Perhaps it had been raining all day at the club. But it hadn't.

A friend of mine had climbed to 17,000. "Where have you been?" he asked. I could have killed him. It's always the day you are working. God's law.

There couldn't be another day like that. Not for years. All the same, the next morning I got my sailplane ready early. I polished the wings. Then I checked everything.

I had no oxygen. It wasn't fixed yet. But there wasn't much hope of needing that, I thought. Not after yesterday.

My publishers had kept me up late. I didn't feel too good. I went off to the club for a coffee.

26

I listened to the forecast. Thunderstorms. Weather forecasts are always wrong. It was dead calm. Useless. No one bothered to fly all morning.

But that afternoon clouds began to form. Good ones. Maybe that forecast was right after all. I took off. "Optimist," someone said.

For a while I thought they were right. I had a job to keep up. At last I got into cloud. It wasn't very high. Don't get lost today, I told myself. You can't see far.

If I did have to land in a field I'd be in trouble. Apart from the rules I didn't have a trailer yet. That would make life very difficult.

Slowly I climbed higher. 6,000 feet. I came out and found the airfield. Then another cloud took me up more quickly. But at 13,000 the lift vanished. I had got excited for nothing.

I flew around. It was cold and dismal. Far below I spotted the club through a hole in the cloud. I wasn't lost. But I was losing height again.

I looked along the wings. Ice. But I was looking at something else. A cloud. *The* cloud.

This cloud looked different. It was bursting out of
the sky. Like a giant mushroom. It rumbled sullenly.
A thunderstorm was coming. A beauty.

It was madness to fly anywhere near it. But I had to
have a go. In I plunged. Bond was right. Some men will
do anything for diamonds.

Inside it was like liquid smoke. Damp. Murky. I could
hardly see my instruments. Still losing height. Then
a huge hidden hand shook the glider till she rattled.
Suddenly I was going up. Fast.

This lift was vicious. It hurled the new sailplane
around like a toy. It threw me about in the cockpit.
But I was climbing like a dingbat. "15,000 feet",
I called on my radio. "16 . . . 17 . . . 18 . . . 19 . . ."
I reached out in my mind for that glittering diamond.

I was laughing. Feeling light-headed with success.
The sailplane was coming down now. Had I done it?
I had to make sure. I banked, looking for more lift.

Whoops. Bad turn. Nose coming up. Trying to loop.
Feeling funny now. Kind of muzzy. Something wrong.
Silly − no oxygen. Diving. Must, must slow her up.

I fumbled for the air brakes. Then I passed out.

13

My head. Something heavy was on it. Still muzzy.
I had come round. Lost a lot of height I bet.
More oxygen down here.

Silence. Darkness. What was going on? Still flying.
My glasses had gone. I couldn't see the instruments.
And what was pressing down on my head? It all felt
strange. Horrible. I had to be spinning. Blind.

Something heavy? It was the top of the cockpit.
I must be upside down as well. I felt dazed. Trapped.

It seemed so easy just to lie there. To let it all
happen. Then I thought of Barbie. I remembered what
she said. *Never give up*. Slowly I pulled my feet back
onto the rudder bars. I began to fight the spin.

Suddenly the heaviness on my head went. I was
winning. Then it was back. Worse than ever. I had
done something wrong. I must be spinning the other
way or something. But I mustn't give up, I thought.
I struggled harder with the controls.

I must not give up.

I struggled. I fought. Nothing happened. I thought
about my parachute. But I wouldn't give up. Not yet.
Blindly I tried once more. Full rudder . . .

She felt different. The right way up. No pressure on
my head. And the cockpit was lighter. There was a
blur of movement in the grey murk ahead.

I couldn't see out. Steam on the inside. Ice on the
outside. I opened a little window in the perspex.
My god – the ground. Level with the nose.

There wasn't time to think. Down with the wheel.
Then I was landing in a big field. Just as well.
I had a lot of speed to get rid of.

She stopped. I staggered out. My glasses were right
up in the nose. With my sun hat, map, sweets and
Parker pen. It must have been quite a spin.

I stumbled across the field to find a phone. Big
drops of water splashed down. I stopped and looked
up for a moment.

There was a flicker of rage. A growl of thunder from
the sullen giant that rumbled in the sky above me.
And I hadn't got a trailer.

14

I had this problem. Not the trailer. We borrowed one.
Not the diamond. My little box said I'd been to
nearly 20,000 feet. It was a jewel box now.

No. The problem was the time I took coming down.
About as long as it takes you to read this far down
the page. Or maybe just a bit further.

Forty-five seconds.

I must have been doing about 500 kph at times. Well
over twice VNE. But how? Why didn't the glider break
up? Why was I still alive?

No sailplane could pull out of that kind of dive.
Not with its wings on. And if I hadn't landed in
a valley I would have been smashed flat anyway.
I should have been dead three times over.

Diamonds are forever, said Bond. And so is death.
20,000 feet in 45 seconds? I had been more than
halfway to heaven – the angels were out to meet me.

Crazy. Impossible. Of course it is. But then like I said,
truth is stranger than fiction. You know what I mean,
Bond? Who is really the ghost? You or me?

© James Webster 1980
Illustrations © Macmillan Education Limited 1980

First published 1980

Published by Macmillan Education Limited
Basingstoke and London

Printed in Hong Kong